Fearless Mary

Mary Fields, American Stagecoach Driver

Tami Charles

illustrated by
Claire Almon

Albert Whitman & Company
Chicago, Illinois

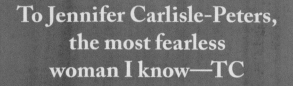

To Jennifer Carlisle-Peters,
the most fearless
woman I know—TC

To my sweet nieces,
all six of them—CA

In the city of Cascade, Montana, Mary Fields sees "Help Wanted" signs everywhere. The city needs a new stagecoach driver to make deliveries to a school, Saint Peter's Mission. It's a good job, an important job, but a dangerous one too.

It's 1895. Sending supplies and messages to Cascade is easy thanks to telegraphs and trains. But the trails that snake through the mountains up to Saint Peter's make it almost impossible to reach.

The best way to deliver the mail there is by stagecoach.

Outlaws prey on stagecoaches, which carry valuable supplies, money, and food. Wild animals prey on them too. The stagecoach is usually guarded by one person: the driver. To do the job, you need to be smart, tough, unshakable.

As a former slave who traveled to the West alone to seek opportunity, Mary Fields is all of those things.

With the job comes respect and high wages—nearly seventy-five dollars a month. With that kind of pay, a person can live a good life. But most people think a job like this is meant for men, not women, and especially not an ex-slave. Getting the job will be hard for Mary. Even though the Wild West is supposed to be a land of opportunity, everything is segregated. "Whites Only" restaurants. "Whites Only" jobs. "Whites Only" pay.

That doesn't stop Mary—it only makes her want to prove that everyone should be equal. Including women.

So the next day, Mary gallops into town, face pointed toward the sky,
ready to take her chance.

At least forty cowboys try out for the job, and Mary steps right up with them.

"We don't hire people like you," the manager says.

Mary stands tall and squares her shoulders. She lived the first thirty-three years of her life without freedom. And now she'd spend the rest of it making sure she got an equal shot at a good life.

HELP WANTED
Stagecoach Driver

"I'm Mary Fields. I can outride any man trying out for this job."
Mary refuses to leave. She waits her turn to show what she can do.

One by one, the cowboys try their best. They swing their lassos, saddle up the horses real fine. But Mary knows she can do that... and more.

So she steps forward again, but the manager points—
"I said not you. You don't belong here."
"I'll show you I do."

And she does.

Mary hitches six horses, cracks her whip, speeds up the hill and back around, the horses' hooves clomping an earthshaking sound. She is a force!

"What's your name again?" the manager asks.

"I'm Mary Fields, but you can call me Fearless!"

No need to look further. The job is hers. No African American woman has ever been hired to drive a stagecoach in Cascade… or in the rest of the country. Mary Fields is the first.

Being "first" is hard. Not everyone likes the idea of a woman driving a stagecoach. Some believe Mary can't do the job, because she is a woman, because of the color of her skin.

But Mary is unbreakable, unshakable.

She travels rugged mountain trails. It's hard to navigate, but Mary can read all kinds of maps including star patterns in the dark sky.

Thieves try to steal from her wagon. Little do they know, Mary's got herself a pet eagle, trained as her faithful protector. They don't stand a chance!

On one moonless night, Mary's wagon hits a gully.
Horse screams pierce the air. Packages fly everywhere.
And a gang of hungry wolves creeps out from the shadows.

Mary's cargo is important: food to feed the school children, letters for loved ones, sent from far away. It's her job to protect her horses and make sure the children at St. Peter's receive their packages.

Mary stands guard all night, iron weapon pressed against her back. With the eagle at her side, she keeps the wolves at bay until the sun rises and chases them away. Mary never loses a single horse or package.

Word of Mary's courage spreads throughout Cascade. She becomes a hometown hero—the stagecoach driver who fended off wolves, trudged through heavy snow, and never missed a single day of work. No task was too small, no task too dangerous. And in time, she would become known as a groundbreaker, a history maker.

Mary rides those trails for eight years, until she is in her seventies.
More women begin to drive stagecoaches and deliver mail across the
United States, fearless like Mary, faces pointed to the sky.

As the years go by, cars, telephones, and airplanes are invented. Delivering the mail becomes easier, less dangerous, and thanks to Mary and others like her, a job held by many women.

Today, Mary's bravery is remembered in Cascade and throughout the country. Delivery men and women still face long days on the road and harsh weather at times, but nothing like the dangers Mary faced in the Wild West.

Every now and then, if you listen closely, you'll hear her voice whispering in the wind: "I'm Mary Fields, but you can call me Fearless!"

Author's Note

One day during Women's History Month, I browsed Facebook and an interesting article appeared in my newsfeed: "Mary Fields Put the 'Wild' in Wild West." The picture showed a woman proudly perched on a stagecoach. The look on her face told a story of hardship and triumph. I *had* to learn more about her.

Finding information about Mary Fields wasn't easy, though the Smithsonian offers great resources about the history of women in the postal service. Many accounts of Mary's life are spotty and conflicting, but all agree that she fearlessly stood up against prejudice and applied for one of the most dangerous jobs in the Wild West. The odds were stacked against her: she was a former slave who still faced racial discrimination, she was a woman, trying out for what many considered a man's job, *and* she was in her 60s!

I wrote *Fearless Mary* to imagine how she earned the job as mail carrier and won the hearts of the people of Cascade, Montana. There's no record of the conversation between Mary Fields and the stagecoach hiring manager, but I based their dialogue on what I've learned about Mary and the resistance she faced as she forged her path. Additionally, Mary's encounter with a wolf occurred before she was hired, back when she worked for the St. Peter's Mission and often ran deliveries through Cascade. But the encounter is a memorable example of the bravery and reliability she was known for as a stagecoach driver.

Mary Fields didn't allow prejudices to hold her back from accomplishing her goals. She is an unsung hero—one whose name should be recognized for all she did and everything she stood for. Mary Fields inspires me to be *fearless*, and I hope she'll do the same for you.

—Tami Charles

Library of Congress Cataloging-in-Publication data is on file with the publisher.

Text copyright © 2019 by Tami Charles
Illustrations copyright © 2019 by Albert Whitman & Company
Illustrated by Claire Almon
First published in the United States of America in 2019 by Albert Whitman & Company
ISBN 978-0-8075-2305-6
Printed in China
10 9 8 7 6 5 4 3 2 1 HH 22 21 20 19 18

Design by Morgan Beck

For more information about Albert Whitman & Company,
visit our website at www.albertwhitman.com.